The Apocalypse of Peter

A Vision of Judgment, Redemption, and Eternity

A Modern Translation

Adapted for the Contemporary Reader

Peter the Apostle

Translated by Tim Zengerink

© **Copyright 2025**
All rights reserved.

It is not legal to reproduce, duplicate, or transmit any part of this document in either electronic means or in printed format. Recording of this publication is strictly prohibited and any storage of this document is not allowed unless with written permission from the publisher except for the use of brief quotations in a book review.

This book contains works of fiction. Any resemblance to persons living or dead, or places, events, or locations is purely coincidental.

Table Of Contents

Preface - Message to the Reader 1

Introduction 5

Apocalypse of Peter 11

Thank You for Reading 17

Preface - Message to the Reader

What If You Could Help Rebuild the Greatest Library in Human History?

Thousands of years ago, the Library of Alexandria stood as the crown jewel of human achievement — a sanctuary where the collected wisdom of every known civilization was gathered, preserved, and shared freely.

And then, it was lost.

Through fire, conquest, and the slow erosion of time, humanity lost not just books — but ideas, dreams, discoveries, and stories that could have changed the world forever.

Today, the Library of Alexandria lives again — and you are invited to be a part of its restoration.

Our mission is simple yet profound:

To rebuild the greatest library the world has ever known, and to translate all timeless works into every language and dialect, so that no seeker of knowledge is ever left behind again.

By joining our movement to rebuild the modern Library of Alexandria, you become part of an unprecedented mission:

- **Unlimited Access to the Greatest Audiobooks & eBooks Ever Written:**

    Instantly explore thousands of legendary works—Plato, Shakespeare, Jane Austen, Leo Tolstoy, and countless more. All instantly available to read or listen, placing a complete literary universe at your fingertips.

- **Beautiful Paperback & Deluxe Editions at Printing Cost**

    Own any title as an elegant paperback, deluxe hardcover, or stunning collectible boxset—offered to you at true printing cost, delivered straight to your door. Build your personal Library of Alexandria, crafted for beauty, built for durability, and worthy of proud display.

- **Fresh Translations for Modern Readers—in Every Language & Dialect**

    Enjoy timeless masterpieces reimagined in clear, contemporary language—no more outdated phrases or obscure references. Alongside the original versions, we're tirelessly translating these classics into every language and dialect imaginable, ensuring accessibility and understanding across cultures and generations.

- **Join a Global Renaissance of Literature & Knowledge**

    You directly support expanding our library, publishing deluxe editions at true cost, translating works into all global languages, and bringing humanity's greatest stories to people everywhere. By joining today, you're not just preserving a legacy of masterpieces; you set in motion a powerful wave of literary accessibility.

Become a Torchbearer of Knowledge.

Join us for free now at **LibraryofAlexandria.com**

Together, we will ensure that the light of human wisdom never fades again.

With gratitude and a shared love of knowledge,

The Modern Library of Alexandria Team

Visit:

www.libraryofalexandria.com

Or scan the code below:

Introduction

A Vision Born from Faith and Fear

In the early centuries of Christianity, believers lived in a world filled with uncertainty, persecution, and moral confusion. Faith was not yet institutionalized, the canon of scripture had not been finalized, and Christian communities existed in tension with both the Roman world and diverse internal interpretations of doctrine. It was during this formative period that texts like The Apocalypse of Peter found their voice. As one of the earliest Christian apocalyptic writings, this remarkable work speaks to the deepest longings of the human heart: the need for justice, the hope for salvation, and the desire to understand what lies beyond the grave.

Attributed to Peter the Apostle and written in the form of a visionary dialogue between Peter and Jesus, The Apocalypse of Peter opens the heavens and the abyss before its readers. It offers a rich, detailed, and often unsettling depiction of the afterlife—one that reflects both the moral urgency and the imaginative power of the early Christian mind. This is not a distant theological treatise. It is a revelation: intimate, visual, and emotional. The righteous are seen in their glory, bathed in light and singing in peace, while the wicked endure punishments that reflect the nature of their sins—fiery, fitting, and unforgettable. Each image serves a purpose, confronting the reader with the reality of divine judgment and the transformative call to live rightly.

But the text is not only about fear. It also offers profound reassurance. For the early Christian struggling to maintain faith under pressure, this vision affirms that God is not silent, that moral choices do matter, and that eternal reward awaits those who remain faithful. It is this pastoral intention that elevates The Apocalypse of Peter beyond simple moralism. The terrifying descriptions of hell are not there to entertain or shock, but to warn and awaken. The beauty of heaven is not there to flatter, but to encourage perseverance. This is a moral map drawn in the language of vision—designed to stir the soul, to provoke reflection, and to guide the conscience toward a holy life.

Although ultimately not included in the official New Testament canon, The Apocalypse of Peter was widely read and respected in the early Church. Some early manuscripts of the Bible included it. Church fathers such as Clement of Alexandria cited it with reverence. And in Ethiopia, it remained part of the religious tradition for centuries. Its popularity testifies to a deep spiritual need it fulfilled—a need that still exists today.

For even in our modern world, with all its distractions and scientific explanations, the questions it raises remain hauntingly relevant: What happens after death? Is there true justice? Does God truly see and respond to human suffering and wickedness?

Judgment, Mercy, and the Moral Imagination

What makes The Apocalypse of Peter so enduring is its ability to combine moral clarity with spiritual vision. Like other apocalyptic texts—such as The Book of Revelation, 1 Enoch, or 2 Esdras—it uses symbolic, often extreme imagery to reveal truths that go beyond ordinary language. Its descriptions of the afterlife are not meant to be literal geography but moral theology in visual form. The punishments of hell are not random or cruel; they are expressions of divine justice. Liars, adulterers, murderers, oppressors—all suffer in ways that correspond to their sins, reinforcing the principle that nothing escapes God's notice. At the same time, the joys of heaven offer a parallel message: that righteousness is not in vain, that love and obedience are seen and rewarded, and that eternal peace is the inheritance of the faithful.

And yet, even in its most terrifying passages, The Apocalypse of Peter hints at something more than strict retribution. In some versions of the text—especially the Ethiopian tradition—the righteous plead with God to have mercy on the damned, and God listens. The prayers of the saints move the heart of the divine. This glimpse of redemptive hope, though subtle and perhaps not present in all manuscripts, adds an extraordinary layer to the message: that mercy is never fully excluded from God's justice. That even the damned are not beyond the reach of divine compassion. This theme resonates with the teachings of Jesus Himself, who spoke of judgment but also of forgiveness, who warned of hell but also called sinners to repentance with love.

This blend of fear and hope, judgment and mercy, is the hallmark of early Christian apocalyptic literature. It does not aim to paralyze the reader with dread, but to jolt them into moral clarity. It challenges the modern reader to consider life not merely in terms of success or failure, pleasure or pain, but in the light of eternity. It invites reflection on the real consequences of our actions, on the state of the soul, and on the kind of person we are becoming. It teaches that the moral order of the universe is not a human invention, but a divine reality—and that to ignore it is to risk everything.

This modern translation has been prepared to make these powerful truths accessible to contemporary readers. Every sentence has been rendered with care, preserving the emotional intensity and symbolic richness of the original while ensuring clarity and readability. The goal is not to dilute the text's impact, but to open the door wider—so that readers from all backgrounds, whether religious or not, can engage with its vision of divine justice and moral urgency.

Reading with the Eyes of Eternity

To truly appreciate The Apocalypse of Peter, it must be read not simply as literature, but as spiritual encounter. It was written to be heard, to be felt, to be remembered. Its words are flames meant to burn away complacency, its images meant to carve themselves into the conscience. Approach it slowly, reflectively. Let it speak to your heart and imagination. Read the descriptions of the righteous and ask: Am I living in a way that leads to such joy? Read the punishments of the wicked and ask: Are there parts of my life that need to change? Let the voice of Peter guide you, not as a distant apostle, but as a witness to a reality more real than anything this world can offer.

Whether you are a Christian seeking deeper understanding, a scholar of early texts, or simply a curious reader pondering the afterlife, this book has something to say to you. It challenges you to see beyond appearances, to live with eternity in view, and to remember that the choices we make now echo forever.

Translated by Tim Zengerink

The Apocalypse of Peter is more than a vision—it is a warning, a promise, and a call. A call to repent, to believe, to love, and to prepare. As you turn the page and enter the world of this vision, may your heart remain open, your conscience awakened, and your hope renewed. Eternity is not far off. It begins now.

Apocalypse of Peter

Many people will claim to be prophets, but they will spread false teachings that lead others down the wrong path. These false teachers will bring destruction upon themselves.

Then God will come to those who remain faithful—those who long for righteousness, endure hardships, and keep their souls pure in this life. He will bring justice against those who live in wickedness.

The Lord then said, "Let's go up to the mountain and pray."

So we, the twelve disciples, followed him. We asked him to show us one of our righteous brothers who had passed away, so we could understand what they were like. We hoped this would give us courage and help us inspire others to believe in our message.

As we prayed, two men suddenly appeared before the Lord, facing the east. Their faces shone as brightly as the sun, and their clothes sparkled with a brilliance beyond anything we had ever seen. Their beauty and glory were indescribable, and we could barely look at them.

We stared in amazement. Their bodies were whiter than the purest snow, yet at the same time, they had a soft red glow, like the petals of the most vibrant rose. The red and white blended perfectly, making them look even more magnificent.

Their curly hair shimmered and flowed over their shoulders like a crown made of fragrant flowers. It reminded me of a rainbow stretching across the sky. Their presence was breathtaking.

They had appeared so suddenly that we were left in complete awe.

I turned to the Lord and asked, "Who are these men?"

He answered, "These are your righteous brothers, the ones you wanted to see."

Then I asked, "Where do all the righteous live? What kind of place is it that gives them such beauty and glory?"

The Lord then revealed a vast and radiant land beyond this world. It was brighter than anything I had ever imagined, filled with pure light, as if the sun itself shone from within it. The air glowed with warmth, and the ground was covered in flowers that never faded, releasing a sweet and refreshing fragrance.

This land was full of beautiful, everlasting plants and trees that produced the most blessed fruit. Even from a distance, the scent of this paradise reached us, filling the air with its heavenly aroma.

The people in this place wore clothes as bright and beautiful as the robes of angels, matching the incredible beauty around them. Angels floated above, making the place even more breathtaking. Everyone there shared the same glory, and they sang together with one voice, praising God with joy.

The Lord said to us, "This is where your high priests and the righteous live."

But then, I saw another place—dark, filthy, and terrifying. It was a place of punishment. The air was thick and heavy, as gloomy as the dark clothing worn by both the punishing angels and those being punished. Some people were hanging by their tongues—these were the ones who had spoken against the righteous path. Beneath them, fire burned, causing them constant pain.

A huge lake of flaming mud was filled with people who had used righteousness for their own selfish gain. Tormenting angels caused them endless suffering. Nearby, women hung by their hair over the bubbling mud. They had dressed themselves to lure others into adultery. The men who had sinned with them hung by their feet, their heads sinking into the filthy, boiling mire.

I thought to myself, "I never imagined such a terrible place could exist."

I saw murderers and their accomplices thrown into a cramped space filled with venomous snakes. The snakes bit them over and over, making them twist and writhe in pain. Dark, crawling worms covered them like a thick cloud, adding to their suffering. The souls of the people they had killed stood nearby, watching and saying, "O God, your judgment is fair."

Not far from there, I saw another tight space where blood and filth from the suffering people drained into a pool, forming a lake. Women sat in the filthy liquid, submerged up to their necks. Across from them sat the children they had conceived but aborted. The children cried out, and sparks of fire shot from their mouths, burning the women's eyes. These were the women who had caused abortions and were now cursed for their actions.

Elsewhere, men and women burned up to their waists in a dark place while evil spirits beat them. Worms ate them from the inside, never stopping. These were the ones who had betrayed and attacked the righteous.

Nearby, some men and women chewed on their own lips in torment while burning irons were pressed into their eyes. They had spoken against righteousness and spread lies. Others bit their own tongues, and fire shot from their mouths—these were the false witnesses.

In another part of this place, sharp, burning-hot stones, sharper than swords, covered the ground. Men and women dressed in torn, dirty clothes rolled on them, suffering without end. These were the rich people who had put their trust in wealth, ignored orphans and widows, and disobeyed God's commands.

In a huge, bubbling lake filled with blood and filth, people stood knee-deep in the disgusting mixture. These were the greedy lenders who charged others unfair amounts of interest.

Others were thrown off a high cliff. When they hit the ground, they were forced to climb back up, only to be thrown down again, never finding rest. These were the men who had dishonored their bodies by acting like women and the women who had lain with each other like a man and woman should.

Next to the cliff, fire burned where men who had made idols for themselves stood, trapped in the flames. Nearby, other men and women carried rods, striking each other over and over without end.

Translated by Tim Zengerink

In another place, men and women burned and twisted in agony. Their bodies roasted in the flames. These were the ones who had abandoned God's way to chase after their own selfish desires.

Thank You for Reading

Dear Reader,

We hope this timeless classic has sparked your imagination and enriched your literary journey. Now that you've turned the final page, we want to share a vision for the future of reading—one where every classic you've ever wanted to explore is at your fingertips, in a format that best suits your life.

We'd like to invite you to gain immediate, unlimited digital & audiobook access to hundreds of the most treasured literary classics ever written—along with the option to secure deluxe paperback, hardcover & box set editions at printing cost. Together, we can spark a new global literary renaissance alongside our small, independent publishing house called "The Library of Alexandria."

Thousands of years ago, the Library of Alexandria stood as a beacon of knowledge—until it was lost to history. We aim to reignite that spirit of preservation and discovery right now, in the modern age—only this time, it's accessible to all, in every language and every format.

Picture a world where every timeless classic, novel, poem, or philosophical treatise is not only available to read but also updated for today's readers—modernized, translated into any language or dialect, and ready to enjoy in any format you choose, whether that is in an eBook, audiobook, paperback, or deluxe hardcover & box set version a printing cost.

By joining our movement to rebuild the modern Library of Alexandria, you become part of an unprecedented mission to offer:

- **Unlimited Audiobook & eBook Access to the Greatest Classics of All Time**

    Instantly explore thousands of legendary works, from Plato and Shakespeare to Jane Austen and Leo Tolstoy. All are instantly ready to read or listen to, giving you a complete literary universe at your fingertips.

- **Paperback & Deluxe Editions at Printing Costs:**

    Purchase any title in a paperback, deluxe hardbound, or deluxe boxset edition at printing costs, shipped right to your doorstep. Curate your personal library of Alexandria with editions worthy of display—crafted to last, designed to captivate, and delivered straight to your door.

- **Modern translations for Contemporary Readers in all languages and dialects**

  Discover a vast selection of classics reimagined in clear, current language—no more struggling with outdated phrases or obscure references. Next to the original versions, we aim to offer translations in as many languages and dialects as possible.

  As we continue our translation efforts and add new languages, readers everywhere can connect with these works as if they were written today. By bridging linguistic divides, you're contributing to ensuring that these timeless stories become more meaningful, accessible, and inspiring for people across the globe.

- **Your Personal Library of Alexandria:**

  Over the months and years, you'll curate a unique physical archive of classics—each volume a testament to your taste, curiosity, and love of knowledge. It's not just about owning books—it's about curating a cultural legacy you'll cherish and pass down for generations to come.

- **Join a Global Literary Renaissance:**

  Your support fuels an ongoing mission: allowing us to reinvest in offering deluxe print editions (including special boxsets) at their true cost, broaden the range of available formats and translations, and extend the reach of these works to new audiences worldwide. By joining today, you're not just preserving a legacy of masterpieces; you set in motion a powerful wave of literary accessibility.

We are more than a publisher—we're a movement, and we can't do it alone. Your support lets us scale our mission, preserving and reimagining history's greatest works for tomorrow's readers.

Become a Torchbearer of knowledge.

Thank you for picking up this book and allowing us into your literary journey. As you turn the pages, know that you're part of something larger: a global effort to keep these stories alive, share their wisdom across borders and generations, and spark a true cultural revival for the modern era.

If this resonates with you—please consider taking the next step by visiting:

www.libraryofalexandria.com

With gratitude and a shared love of knowledge,

The Modern Library of Alexandria Team

Visit:

www.libraryofalexandria.com

Or scan the code below:

www.ingramcontent.com/pod-product-compliance
Lightning Source LLC
LaVergne TN
LVHW030632080426
835512LV00021B/3472